I0764610

Solitary Bee

SOLITARY BEE

Poems by

Chelsea Woodard

Measure Press
Evansville, Indiana

Printed in the United States of America
First Edition

The text of this book is composed in Baskerville.
Composition by R.G.
Manufacturing by Ingram.

Woodard, Chelsea
Solitary Bee / by Chelsea Woodard — 1st ed.

ISBN-13: 978-1-939574-18-3
ISBN-10: 1-939574-18-8
Library of Congress Control Number: 2016914823

Measure Press
526 S. Lincoln Park Dr.
Evansville, IN 47714
http://www.measurepress.com/measure/

Acknowledgments

The author wishes to thank the editors of the publications in which these poems have appeared, sometimes in slightly different forms.

32 poems: "Whale Song"
American Arts Quarterly: "Keeping Bees"
Blackbird: "Midwinter"
The Dark Horse: Scottish-American Poetry Magazine: "The Casket Maker"
The Iron Horse Literary Review: "Lupines"
Measure: "The Swimming Hole" and "Things We Inherit"
Mezzo Cammin: "The Bat"
New South: "Wedding Day"
Shenandoah: "Solitary Bee"
The Threepenny Review: "Our Swords"

for my parents

CONTENTS

I. Line

II. Range

III. Flight

IV. Return

"In burrows narrow as a finger, solitary bees
keep house among the grasses. Kneeling down
I set my eyes to a hole-mouth and meet an eye
round, green, disconsolate as a tear."

— Sylvia Plath, "The Beekeeper's Daughter"

I. Line

Our Swords

When I was five, I found my father's sword
collection piled clanging in a heap,
forgotten in a corner. Blade on board,
they rested, rusting in the attic's keep.
Midwinter slanted pale across the stored-
up dust: slow floating bullets without sound.
I knelt inside the silent cold. The ground

became a vane for light, a gesture of
December's afternoon that pointed *here*,
to these sharp edges I now loomed above,
the wars and generations I wiped clear
once I had claimed them. Peeling off the glove
of my inheritance, I shuddered, felt
the Civil War — a tarnished metal belt

I strapped against my tiny hips. I let
the scabbard graze my skin, and thought I could
be brave among these prairie ghosts I'd met
in stories. Here, I shared their blood. I stood
among my kinsmen, staring at a set
of slashed out lives — the rest I'd never known.
Twelve blades: each month could have its own

relic to remind us what we'd turned to since:
to pacifists and boys who dodged the draft,
sad drunks who lost their land — cut down to glints
of dulling steel — we'd waste it all. A shaft

of feeble light: our shortest day imprints
itself in crust-topped snow. Inside, I bent
above our swords, and dragged one as I went.

Things We Inherit

for my father

That day he couldn't do it. Walking back
across the grass, his brother held a gun.
The dog trailed after, keeping to the wall.
My father watched his father down a shot
of something smoky, bitter. Ochre fields
turned sparrow brown. They didn't go to church.

The priest sat staring at the rain. The church
was cold and everyone had left — gone back
to Sunday's quiet hours, flooded fields
and washed-out roads where someone hid a gun
behind a split-rail fence. My father shot
a rubber band that bounced back off the wall

and dropped. He heard his parents through the wall.
His mother yelled she would have *joined the church,*
his father slurred her father *would have shot*
him if he knew. Some things you can't take back —
the boy's all grown — and outside there's a gun
wrapped in a cotton shirt; it guards the fields

against the dark. My father crossed his field
of vision on fogged glass. He felt the wall
between the house and night, forgot the gun
his brother carried, looking for a church
key for his father's beer. His mother backed
inside the kitchen, looking at a shot

in black and white — the four of them. She shot
a glance outside, and saw the crying fields
the water on the window made. Way back
when she was young she balanced on a wall
and spread her arms like wings and wished the church
could hold her weight. She didn't know the gun

her eldest kept. He woke, picked up the gun.
The light-filled morning didn't hear the shot.
My father's mother rose and went to church.
My father ran across the bladed fields.
The priest leaned against the sun-warmed wall
and wondered *how could anyone come back*?

The church is shrouded over burning fields.
My father hides the gun and swallows the shot.
The wall lies stone by stone and doubles back.

Hide and Seek

The Windsor Place, Cape Cod

The nails stick through the closet wall,
and there are voices calling
down the wind-railed corridors.
Remember you once scored
your name into the graying slats,
followed the shadow's flat,
memory's dim, prickling design.
Salt crusts the dock's high water line.

I crouch in wait for age's footsteps
on the stair, finger the ragged letters
in the corner that still tends
the dust-mote quiet; suspend
each hour to drift and splinter harshly
as the hiding child's plea: *find me.*

Donner Summit

The last three would have frozen in the pass —
midnight, blizzard, too dark to see.

My father grew up in its shadow, tracing
water rings from bottles skiers left

half-emptied on the wooden tables in the lodge.
His parents owned the ranch for seven years

before it got to them — began to gnaw
like teeth, dull on frozen bread crust, like rust

wearing the steel clamps thin on the lifts
they'd need to replace before next year's first snow.

The storms came sudden there, grabbed each frail
morning by its slender neck, jaws locked, ready

to break it. His father — engineer and alcoholic — built
a motor for the plow truck, then disassembled all its parts;

he couldn't beat it, give it up. He'd use the shovel's
flat to scrape a path out to the car so he could leave, take

along my father to play cards on a barstool, drink
Pepsi in mid-morning, his brothers off at school.

Below the mountain, the jukebox hummed
its lazy tune in the dim grime of the bar, and the whiskey

burned, as warm as any fire could in the cold.
The dark peak had been a beacon for the party — lost,

with no stars to steer by through the maze of snow.
A little boy, my father drained the last dregs

from a bottle, liked the stale beer, sour, nobody
looking. Afternoons he played cops and robbers

with a migrant boy who lived in the shacks
below the ranch. They claimed empty boxes

in a garbage heap, took turns guarding the discarded
metal scraps and car parts, pair-less shoes.

A boy could die there — suffocate on any evening
if a snowdrift pitched and trapped him, his small cries

muffled by the hill. It should have been easy to forget
the choking dark — with skiing, sled dogs, blinding

light on snow. Their family tried to but it didn't catch.
The truck stalled when it was too cold, and at night

the gales cried off the porch, the huskies' barks hard
at the wood door. Each taut sleep waited, dreamless,

for the crunch of boots in snow, a stranger's knock,
a figure in the dark pass, leading the way out.

Ides

There is a flock pecking around
the crab apple outside. I hear
their fretful *gobble.* The tom's perched
on a low and trembling branch.
I watch the snow drip to the ground,
wait for the dog to bark,
the heavy scene to topple.

Gizzards boil in a black pot
on my mother's stove.
It is a German thing, she says,
to eat of all the parts.
The flesh is sinewy and firm.
She cuts small bites for me sprinkled
with crushed thyme leaves, pepper and salt.

In Latin class our teacher asked
us to arrange the month into three
sets of days. It is the middle I remember,
when the gold changed hands.
My mother wore an old coin
as a pendant on a thin, filigree chain.

The Romans read their fortunes
in the flights of birds, but I can't guess
what these bare tree limbs auger;
the glutted flock's gone toward the woods,
but every March I see the outline

of their awkward bodies still —
the muddy ground marking
their place; the boughs emptied
and scratching at the house all of these years
like a reminder of forgotten debts.

Roman Coin

Your father bought it from a market vendor
near Viterbo, north of Rome. He saved
it in a square of silk, and gave it to you
for your birthday. He said it was *for luck*.

Now, you wear it as a pendant, charm,
or talisman — the profiled head obscured
from sweat-damp skin and centuries. You think
the face is Nero, imagine it's worth thousands,
like those unearthed a few years back
in London, still intact in leather pouches,
dropped by a lady, senator, or maid.

You ask me when I intern at the auction house
one summer to do research, find its value,
but having little proof, I only offer
yes, that it is old, probably Nero;
it may have survived the fire in Rome.
I assure you I am certain
you could sell it, sure that it's worth something.

Despite your questioning, I know the coin
will ornament the recess of your breasts,
your jewelry box, the safe you had
installed in case of fires, not trusting banks
to keep what things you treasured most.

In Sicily, you once found a perfect half
of calyx in the dirt by Hera's temple —
overlooked by other tourists, excavators.
You wrapped it in your scarf to show
the site keepers and me; my siblings
hidden behind scattered, trunk-less pediments.

I thought that you had turned it in, but last year
I stood behind you as you opened up
the safe, showing me the combination
just in case you said, and underneath
the stacks of letters, our inheritance
of pearls, deeds to the unkempt property,
I saw a bundle in a bright red scarf —
it was the one you wore that day we climbed
under relentless sun, the silk tied, garish, in your hair.

Glinting brief moments in the light,
the pendant weighed like stone upon your chest
as you mined toppled structures for a shard
of glass or gold — some remnant indiscernible
as one emperor's eroded likeness on the coin's face.
Distorted over years, the metal
gleams, as unexpected as a fire
or shelter from it — nearly impossible
to catalog or ever know its worth.

Lesson

I. Gesture

It's what they teach you first — to map
a motion in a single line.
From the atlas to the heel,
I dragged my brush across the page
to catch the temper of a practiced slouch.
A single line can tell you where
the weight is carried, how the spine
adapts the spirit of a pose.

The light and shadow speak of other things.
I store my drawings in a stack
that, leafed through quickly like a flip-book,
will reveal one movement's story —
how a body arches brightly first
before it stoops and straightens, walks away.

II. Perspective

Project each line to where it disappears.
The building tops at first recede
too sharply, and the figures in the foreground
loom unreasonably tall. Inside
the chapel walls, the early master
still endures the damp; the fresco's
cracks, spreading like lattice, fail to dull
his perfect scale. He worked, relentless,

for a year, then left. When he returned,
I wonder if the picture seemed
at once mysteriously clear: the figures
and grand cities now distilled,
each fold of cloth and crumbled pediment
explained, converging somewhere past the flat, gray hill.

III. Form

Each body lends itself to variation.
The pears lining the windowsill
appear, this morning, to be leaning slightly
toward the sun. The crocus buds,
shrugged closed now in the dewy cold, mirror
their egg-shaped bulbs. I pulled the thick
down blanket back, and let the light decide
the volume of his face, asleep,

one side still masked in dark. Easy to miss
is how each element conspires
to shape the whole: how shadows crowd
in every cleft, the sunlight snagging
bristled skin; the way you learn to render
weight resisting motion, lines you cannot bend.

Family Portrait

Swan Lake, Montana, 1930
i.m. James Woodard

Even in this, your chin lifts stiffly to stand
up to the camera lens. Your feet are bare.
On your thin shoulder rests her stony hand.
Into the dropping sun, your mother's glare

fears day has gone for good. The tamarack
stretches its limbs above your sunburned heads.
The picture doesn't catch the sudden crack
as lightning hit; kids, dreaming in your beds,

only in morning saw the fallen branch
breaking the yard in half. Your mother knew
it couldn't last. She sold the family ranch
three years after your brother died, and you

grew sullen, still clinging to her apron folds.
The hand holding the camera points and scolds.

Two Scenes

I.

"Let's clean this up before your mother comes."
Your father wraps the body in a quilt.
You help him dig a hole. A deerfly hums

while you tramp roses, wreck a plot of mums,
and bear your bone-white brother, and the guilt.
Best clean this up before your mother comes

to weed the garden. A hand, cold as a hoe's claw, plumbs
the soil to cleave the root. The flowers wilt
while you help plant the spattered clothes. A deerfly hums

II.

above the preacher's head, and whiskey numbs
the body from the keener's awful lilt.
You'll clean this up before your mother comes

to find the truck and liquor gone. Rain drums
its sorrow on the metal roof. The future tilts
because you helped him dig that hole. A deerfly hums

the newscast's suicide, and spoils a crate of early plums.
You spill the fruit, and break the box you built,
but clean it up before your mother comes.
You helped him dig the hole. A deerfly hums.

Dream of Bees

The tower's hidden by the trees.
Time's clanging from a copper bell.
One stroke before the last one fell,
I followed on a yellow breeze.

I visited the homes of bees,
the way I know I'll never tell.
The tower's hidden by the trees.
Time's clanging from a copper bell.

The flowers know the coming freeze
and hang their dust: a quiet spell.
My honey-face smiles from a well.
The clapper stops; the hand agrees.
The tower's hidden by the trees.

II. Range

Syringa Vulgaris

for a friend

When you were born your mother lost her voice.
The graves were quiet under heavy snow,
the oaks forgiving as the day slid low
between their frozen boughs. She made a choice
to come here — leave the city for a man
and miles of scrubby brush and storm-bent trees.
Your mother never taught you how to please
somebody, smooth a sheet down flat, or plan
a marriage that would keep. She spent a season
by her window, draped in wool to blot the light.
Her fingers cracked and bled from cold. At night
she let your father in, or found a reason
to hoard her silence in an empty room —
sun trapped inside a glass, a lilac's bloom.

Shearing Season

My mother walked ahead of me.
I trailed along the furrowed mud
in purple galoshes.
She said I was to be polite.
I looked around, discovering
a lost country in the old tractors
and white plastic covered hay bales,
the bleating lambs, low rough-edged outbuildings,
and silos reaching up like obelisks
to pierce the storm-gray April sky.

We came to see the lambs.
The farmer's wife had told us
just a minute. I watched her sitting
at her loom, her feet almost invisible
in clouds of wool that she would card
and smooth for spinning spools of thread.
The barn door gaped
onto the rain-soaked field that was rock-strewn,
sparsely covered with new grass.
I bent down, timid, and slipped
past the women like a cast off stitch.
In the pasture, the lambs clustered
by the stone wall, heads buried
in each other's wooly hindquarters,
until it was their turn.

The farmhand grabbed them
by their wobbly legs. He held
the shears like splayed silver fingers
and clipped the fleece into a drift
that spread across the bleary landscape.
The lambs were held down, hooves bound
and sticking skyward, brown eyes
rolled back. I turned and ran from them,
a tuft of fleece curled tight inside my small fist;
feet squelching in the wet ground.

Posting Land

In late November I would hear them
coming up the road: old trucks creeping
at a stalker's pace, scanning
leafless trees for the slender forms
of deer — now frozen still to blur
among the lines of trunks
with stick-legs, their bodies
round with winter coats.

Once I helped my mother
put the signs up on our trees —
flimsy yellow paper bans.
We worked in the cold
without talking. In the distance,
a gunshot broke the quiet.
It echoed from the valley,
the violet hillsides, the fir trees
that hid the ruffled feathers
of the birds — hushed, waiting.

I didn't wonder about our vigilance.
I pictured the saddle-colored deer
running over snow, the way they nosed
for apples in the still-gray morning,
safe beneath the heavy boughs
beyond the house and paddock,
the frozen fields; their breath
like smoke, our wood stove

burning low as we settled down
like apple-ash into our beds, lost
wandering our winter dreams.

I didn't question then
what we protected as we balanced
on the hard-packed snow
and tacked our leaf-like warnings
to the dark trees, listening
for the diesel rumbling
of a white Ford scouting out another
snowy hilltop, or a field
they hope we have forgotten.

Bluebead Lilies

> *"The plant grows in the shade about the edges of swamps. The berries, which are of a peculiar dark, indigo blue grow in umbels of two or five on the summits . . . . they are rather rare and known to few . . . . toward the end of August they are mostly fallen."*
>
> — Thoreau, *Wild Fruits*

Our parents told us not to eat them.
They said that they were *poison* —
that they could make a full-grown man lie
bone flat, choking himself blue
in the trampled dirt.

They'd tried to make us recognize
the difference — the deadly berries
from those common ones clumped
on the low, snaggy bushes at the edge
of the neighbor's dew-slicked grass, the ones
I snuck out early to pick before
the beagle woke up on the screen porch
next door and gave me away.

The sapphire-colored berries looked
like heaven — smooth and plump,
with a round, split swell.
We knew they wouldn't last.
In a few weeks, they would fall
to the wet moss, stealing their blue shine
that had held my siblings and me in its spell.

The lily's berries grew on straight, slender stalks.
They peeked up much too eager from the rest
of the brush and saplings skirting the sides
of the path that traced the water's edge,
the one that led us running, breathless,
early each morning while the berries hummed
thick, beneath the drowned trees, waiting.

My siblings took the wild berries
by the handful — rolling them up into their shirts
until the cotton stained through purple —
their swelling bellies white
against the settled fog and the lake's glassy smile.

I waded through the dark leaves, feet bare, aching
for the fruit. I bent above the wicked, bead-like heads,
thinking, if I plucked one, how the bitter juice
would sting my tongue, dye my fingers
deep violet, and make them trembling, strange.

I wondered how long it would take,
if I'd be able to swallow,
how the lake would look turned upside down —
our faces poured like water from the sky.

Free-Range Cattle

That spring, Bill Taylor's cows preferred
our front lawn to their mountain pasture.
I woke to their bells in the fog. I dreamt of the herd
breaking trail on the ridge in the last
bit of dark, bony-backed, as they clambered
through bramble and pine to our margin of grass.

In the yard, they were awkward and huge:
brown-white giants who eyed me with mistrust
when, barefoot, I walked where they grazed
afternoon hours in the shade of the locust.
We never got word they were lost,
but at dusk, a whistle came from the hill,

and the farmer's wife shook a bucket of grain.
The cattle turned toward the sound, and filed
slowly back to the trees they had come from.
Tired of restringing barbed-wire, Bill
sold the herd to a friend whose fields
bordered the river. Miles of mossy, green

banks served as fence, but the cows were at home
in no pasture. They filled their bellies, then took
the current downstream for new range. We combed
the tall grass for dried dung, muddy tracks;
scoured the distance for bells, for light clinging to wet flanks.

Snow

We thought it unremarkable, how world
would cover world — fields overcome by white,
neatly raked leaves and brush-pile towers sunk
for months, for good it seemed. We welcomed light

that almost blinded us, remembered days
with sound cut out, toughened our skin to cold.
Resigned to read a cool spectrum of blues,
we didn't miss the darting flecks of gold

caught on the water when we rowed. The river
gurgled even beneath thick ice, swirled black
against the fishermen's drilled holes. Recklessness,
too, disguised as child's play, until a crack

shattered the winter's spell — the only sound
making us clutch and shiver on the ground.

Hot Air Balloons

Like sleeping dragons, the balloons
stretched half inflated on the field.
The pilot was getting coffee, the crew
untying ropes, checking the envelope
for tears. The propane flared like sunlight
on my father's sleeve as they lifted off,
hot blasts wrinkling the morning air.

Later, in a car with strangers, I traced
the red swell of balloon floating
above the hills, blotting their flight
out with my thumb. I wouldn't take
my father's hand, standing instead
to eye the wicker basket from the grass,
fists cold and stuck inside my pockets.

Balloons landed in roadside pastures
every fall, scaring cows, making
carloads of tourists stop to gawk.
I feared the geese would freeze
gliding all night on gelid ponds,
wheeling for miles across the roof
of clouds, the flaring maple tops.

Each September, from the interstate, I see
the bright dots hanging in the blue
like magic ships, my sister waving
as the bucket lifts, each breath

taking them farther, making me crane
back, flightless and shaking
on the sweep of frost to watch.

Widow-Makers

The name is a surprise the first time
my father explains what they are called.
Hanging like heavy wire sculpture
high above the class-three road, these snagged
hazardous scraps from wind storms
grimly usher us beneath them.

I think maybe there are harder ways,
recalling how his father died alone inside
that smoke-filled cabin, how the ice broke
underneath the fishing shacks one year —
church spires sticking the metal sky,
the hills rust-tinged and wrung with bells.

A red-tailed hawk has made her nest
high in a white pine fifteen yards ahead.
She's used the deadfall as a base,
and guards her new clutch fiercely,
puffing her speckled breast as we pass by.
Her gaze, yellow as stargrass, tracks us.

Brush and new saplings snap as we tramp
where the town hasn't kept up the road.
Hunting voles, the tiercel screeches
through the woods, and swoops. A dead limb
loosens, falling with a clatter, then a crash.
A woman's pale eyes sift the sky and ash.

The Senator Frye

Each evening as the sun begins to slouch
toward Bemis Mountain, and trout
rise in silver flicks to swallow mayflies
in the calm, the neighbors take
their Chris-Craft for a turn
around the lake. My mother watches
from the dock. She loves
to see the pink light lapping the wooden hull,
the prim bow cutting the surface
like a blade. She has wanted
to ride with them in the boat for years, but never asks.

This is the scene that I remember:
twilight washing the faded porch, my father
pulling sails out of a drawer, rigging
our little boat, the shoreline sharp
with skipping rocks, a loon's dot
on the water, jets groaning east
above us toward ocean, pine pitch
stuck to our skin, splinters from driftwood
we'd collect, *The Senator Frye*'s wake
parting the mirrored dusk in waves.

Viewed from the lake, our cabin's roof
slumps under birches, shingles peeling,
porch lattice wrecked by dogs.
My mother hates to swim, but will not
ask this favor of our neighbors.

Sunfish

On the boat, I think you'll ask me why
I came home late, missed
cherry cobbler, our cribbage game.
We look out over the bow
at the stiff-ridged waves ripping
to the southwest in a cool wind.
I go with you since I can remember.
It's August, gusty afternoon.
Blueberries crowd on low bushes,
and the birch trees shine frayed
paper trunks in late sun, singing leaves.
You knew I'd come along,
and not my brother — only son — who'd stick
to porch shadows, humming Dylan,
fingers strung against the fretboard
of the pale wood Gibson we found
in the cabin's attic. Our mother
hadn't claimed it, pushed it back
to red-crushed velvet, a case
with latch-rust, a wish to keep shut.

A boy's hands would be better
for the lines, the sheets — the rough-
grained rudder I push down once
we've reached the end of the dock.
Boats are more a boy's distraction —
better than girls or cars, fury's burn.
I get splinters. My hands are too small,

too soft for tacking fast
or leaning out from the jib line
when we heel hard, and I have to trust
that you won't tip us — sails, rope,
bailing bucket, your aviator glasses,
the life jackets we'd have
if we hadn't left them on shore,
too certain of the day's turn,
practiced muscle, wood hull, wind.

I'm seventeen. I can't tell you what
I've done. The lake water's cold
on the one hand I let drag the surface
like a fin, cutting ripples in dark waves,
and I remember the boy's hair — starless
water — my fingers through it, how
he lifted me on rough dock slats, light as a sail.
I held my breath until the sky blurred
into his hair and the night fled
from around us, stilled in leaves.

Here, the sun glints from the rocky edges
of the far shore, like it knows what I don't.
We've stopped talking, and let
gusts and hull on water fill the quiet.
The wind shifts, and you ask me
if I want to steer. I take your place
in the stern, and point us north
toward the river's mouth, where I know
the loons are nesting and the trout leap
high in mornings for the Grey Ghost fly.
The mares' tails flush pink with dusk,

and I can't tell you how it all looks different:
how the sail divides the landscape into two parts,
that I'll never feel the keel's tilt lurch
in my stomach, how in darkness I will wait
for the loon's call, alone on the lake,
and search for its body in daylight
from the low boat in order to know
where it hides, in what shelter, what warmth.

A Place to Land

for Dawson

I only wanted us to drive until
        the barking stopped —
until I couldn't see the faded
        sides of hills that closed us in,
or dad's old tractor taking up the yard.
        We drove to where our family acres thinned —
out past the pine trees that we'd traded
        for our happiness, for means that couldn't fill
the empty space. The ground was frozen hard.
        The sun had dropped.

You asked if I remembered gathering
        the leaves, the way
we made a pocket from your shirt,
        and chased each other on the grass
that hugged the road. You reached out your tiny hand
        to trace the "V" of geese, the last
one far off, lagging. "Is he hurt?"
        Your voice was still too new; I couldn't bring
myself to break the sky, this tree-bare land
        we'd turned to hay.

III. Flight

Solitary Bee

> *". . . Eighty-five percent of bees are solitary — meaning a single female mates with a male and then constructs, provisions, and lays an egg in each cell in a nest by herself . . . . Solitary bees do not produce honey or wax, are relatively docile and not apt to sting."*
>
> — from the National Biological Information Infrastructure

She builds her small apartment in a hollow
reed, or tunnels underground. She makes
no honey, but collects the lilac's nectar
for her single brood. The garden stakes
frame her reticulum of flight: like knives
they caution rashness, keep her from the hive's
thick humming in the apple tree outside.

The throat can close or gape: she'll follow
where the gardener weeds and sows the beds
of foxglove, poppy, rose. A flower's bride,
the bee maintains her pattern, flies unwed
to any yearning, colony, or drone. She has
no sting, but still the other bees will shun her,
swarm, and guard their combs like jealous wives.

Amaryllis

We watched it open from the wet earth,
disbelieving its white petals after weeks
of thick green stem overwhelming the planter,
leaves arching upward, bent back,
tips touched low to the wood floor. I knew
the position, had known for some time
the feigned lightness of that grace —
an *arabesque*, a *port de bras* — dipping back
just enough for it to look real, hold the space,
not quite break you. My vertebrae resisted
the firm hand's push down, my teacher straight
at my bent side, testing how far I'd make it.

It took eight weeks for only one blossom.
We planted the bulb — you, hesitant to help
nestle it in black dirt, your big hands clumsy
with its brown, papery skin, the unexpected weight
heavy in your palm. I filled the rest in, buried
the hard swell and tender shoots, pale
at the top. All we had to do was wait,
watering only when it grew — a discipline
of movement carefully measured against
another's. At times the motion was too delicate,
too tempting to betray. I overwatered the bulb,
afraid it would grow dry by the window, the light
too glaring, too harsh at midday.

You thought we should leave it, give
it just enough to find its way up from the dark.
It'll come when it's ready, you said, and my hoping
wouldn't change it. It was March, and I waited
six more weeks with snowmelt dripping
from the eaves and spots of wet ground
growing wider, showing brown lawn, bringing
birds. The bud broke open overnight, spread
its broad petals toward the glass. I wanted
to mistrust the flower — snow-white petals splayed,
perfectly supported from below. It grew from light
and water, black soil, scaled resolve.
I couldn't match its grace, and bent too far
in my last pose, losing my balance when you leaned
close — the form this time too painful to fake.

Starlings

No meadows here, or gardens overgrown,
weed-choked and wrecked with bramble; here,
no barred owl tracks his passage under ranks of pines
or hunts the night-dark marsh for voles burrowed
in matted grass. Instead, the new, moon-whitened furrows
thread the town like worry lines

across the face of one who waits
for spring — the slow, pheromonal pull of mates
tired of their wintering in vacant rooms
that open now, the way expectant mouths
strike from their cornices for fleshy scraps,
or buds, loosened in sunlight, bloom.

The surest sign of April here, amid the caterwaul
of strays, is the forsythia, thrusting tawny stalks
through pavement cracks and fenced-in yards;
its light, beneath the bluish glow of street lamps, smolders.
Like bustles crushed in chatter, or bevies of girls
bunched in the hall, the city birds crowd

oaks in parking lots, as if none but the loudest
will be picked to sweep across the parquet, twirling.
The only quiet to be found rests
in last season's husks — trees still and bare,
free from this desperate, trilling air —
the mocking stares of unbuilt nests.

The Casket Maker

He keeps his shop behind the house,
and mans his booth at local trade shows
on the weekends. His wife tries her best
not to complain of loneliness, and allows
herself the company of borrowed
children, grown, who've come to guess
what shape would suit their mother's frame.

He's almost finished with a box
for Larry — owned the grocery store —
and with her age, the mortgage, and the funeral costs,
his widow will likely have to close before
the spring. The craftsman sands each panel
smooth, and bevels corners for a perfect fit.
He eases the lid down when he's done,

and locks it tight over the chalky faces
of the little town whose dead will keep
his wife in clip-on pearls and pay
the water bill. He defends his craft
as service, but sometimes the axe slips,
misses his thigh by an inch, and he's not sure.
He chooses apple wood, and birch with burls

that his hand and band saw hew to polished rings.
Every evening after dinner, he goes out to build
clean walls against the dark. His clients never know the hours
he bears alone, his shop light

blinking through the midnight trees. He brings
along a cup of coffee, hopes his powers
work this time, that the grain will split right.

Post and Beam

From here, there isn't anyplace to go.
Back home, the record flips and static crackles

from the soft, black speakers that are standing
as they did when I was six, shoring cobwebs

in the corners of my parents' living room.
My father's playing Pavarotti, maybe the Beatles

out of a drawer full of old vinyls
that he'll sometimes take out, but never give up

to old record stores or to my brother
who might like them. That living room's no longer

mine, if it was ever. Here, my hardwood floors
are new, and rented; they don't bear any

of the scars of those old log-singed, dog-scratched slats
inside the house that perches, white, on granite ledge

above the pines. I have no worthy cause for my complaint:
there have been no chimney fires here,

no thankless children wrecking cars or swearing
at their mother; no thirty years of work

at love, tracing rough umber burls with unsure hands,
awkward along the blemishes

that like the fire's black you cannot ever scrape clean.
The Yankee builders used hemlock or pine

with tall, thick trunks, a coarser grain.
The farmhouse beams hold hatchet marks

showing each cut of how they fell.
In my apartment, repainted moldings speak

of former tenants, like old lovers' names
we might let slip in conversation — small dents and scrapes

that management by now has sanded, polished down.
I wish I cared more for the structure than the belly —

a steady mind before the heart.
It took two days to build the house's frame,

one quarter of the town. Two hundred years
before my parents, the farmers raised the joists

with pulleys, locked them firm with wooden pegs.
The Cape still rests on sloping rock, clings

to its foundation of dry stone. I cannot linger
where the others built, make hold in footing

I don't own. Instead I balance on the purlin
of a borrowed roof after love's last attempt

has scorched the lower floors and cooled to smoke.
My parents will soon sell, and newlyweds

will come and gut the frame for renovations,
strip it back to bare wood planks and sky.

I'd like to ask the early builders how it felt
to raise a skeleton in all that air, to know

by mishap that they could burn it down,
fail where they had loved the most,

that it might weather sleet and fire to bear up generations —
each hand-cut beam fixed, sturdy, to its post.

Term Abroad

"As for Lucy and Cecil, for whom the temple was built, they also joined in the merry ritual, but waited, as earnest worshippers should, for the disclosure of some holier shrine of joy."

— E.M. Forster, *A Room with a View*

Our view was of the building wall across
the street, the still-damp shirts hanging to dry
on sun-drenched lines, geraniums in pots
cracked from the heat, a shard of sky.

Signora made our beds, opened the shutters
wide so we could see. But light only displayed
our mismatched sheets and dirty hair, our blistered
feet. The white, crisp postcard edges frayed

soon with our dragging hems through galleries
and leather-scented shops. By rote, we learned
to ask in this new tongue, beguile and tease
louche strangers as we walked. The river churned

inside its lavish banks: gray-green, chalky and slow.
The streets cradle our laughter's toll, the church bells' echo.

Auberge de Jeunesse

Cork, Ireland
Avec mes souvenirs, j'ai allumé le feu . . .
— Edith Piaf

Marie brushed the sidewalk orange
when she rushed out, late again
into the cold morning drizzle,
her scarf's wave hanging in the doorway,
Her flute-like *au revoir!* floating
on the draft she caught to take her
down the hill past St. Finbarr's stone church,
her black hair raked by the raw March wind.

Here, I'd found accents splashed
like puddles we avoided.
My flatmate Juanma's real name had five parts.
It sounded like an Andalusian cavalry
charging at the Alhambra — the red-walled
beacon of the city he longed for, requesting
each night that we be quiet
so that tomorrow he could finish the schooling
he'd named his *career,* an education
he had stretched to age twenty-five, avoiding
its end like the driving license test
he admitted being too afraid to take.
He'd never had a job, and wrote letters
in a child's hand to a girl back home
he planned to marry, though he didn't love her.
He spent each night in the frosted bedroom
of a Russian girl who lived across the river.

She had pale eyes and straight, straw hair
that fell into her face, the same face I pictured
each time I picked up the phone
and listened to his girlfriend's worried accent
skipping syllables like the half-truths
I tripped over, running out of words
to fill up the space at the other end of the line.

We had a small, red kitchen, and a garden
at the back that we never used.
We lived in whitewashed walls
that separated colors like a prism, translated
footfalls and sighs as if the language didn't matter.

Marie practiced flamenco in the hallway.
She picked ripe apples from the air
that was heavier here somehow,
always waiting for the next rain.
She'd argue that all of the green brought bad luck,
drawing an imaginary sword from her side
and holding it up like a challenge
to the brown patch of grass
we'd never see grow before we left.

Outside, the rain started up again.
I knew at ten o'clock, Juanma
would *make the dinner*, call his girlfriend,
and croon bits of Lorca over the phone,
the words perfect on his tongue
and more earnest than anything
he came up with on his own.
I heard Marie singing in the kitchen,

fashioning a *tarte aux poirots*
from wilted leeks and frozen rashers
she'd had to substitute for *jambon*.
She hummed a song I knew well
from a record playing in the house
where I grew up, across the ocean, inside a kitchen
with wood floors where a woman swayed,
drying the dishes with her back to me.
I remembered the voice, like cigarette smoke
swirled thick around the vinyl —
C'est payé, balayé, oublié . . .

Inside the white room, I watched the water
run off from the eaves into the gutter.
The voice in the kitchen sang out clear,
the notes not belonging anywhere, to anyone.
I thought of paper-thin wings, flashing bright
against a half-lit sky, and a strange girl's face
smiling sadly, turned away so that I couldn't see.

Civil War Reenactment

Our teacher split the class in two, and said that I was to be
Grant, my best friend, Lee, the two of us pigtailed, directing

left, right, left across the baseball field, our voices
booming from the megaphones, whispering

strategy in cool, linoleum-tiled rooms as we hunched
at our desks, our bodies slight as boys', our roles

ill-fitting as the uniform, blue buttoning
from shoe to chin, my hat too big, veiling my eyes.

To make it real, we had imagined moves onto a board like chess:
each of us posed as woman-king, the squares labeled

Antietam, Bull Run, Gettysburg. We formed our characters
from snapshots, devoured textbooks with unprecedented hurry.

I combed my hair like Grant's, practiced the name *Ulysses*
with my pen, my ear drunk on its sibilance, its myth, already sound-struc

To make it real, there had to be a spy, and so another girl, brown ponytai
and braces, sold
us out — rendered the whole war in reverse — pointing my eyes

to where I'd never been, to where, years later, I would visit
on a boyfriend's arm — some Yankee darling — not to be trusted, still n

forgiven that defeat, his heart strange to me then, and still
as distant as the city yard yoked with wisteria,

his vowels coaxing and slow, though never meant to stay.

Before The Solstice

St. Petersburg

We sucked the air out of the afternoon
and locked the door. He didn't want to wait
until the weather cleared, and so we huddled,
small, against the church sides for the sun.

Here, each figure is perfected — tree-straight,
with painted lips, bit red. I walk, heavy-footed,
through this city that's been strangled by a scarf.
Inside my room, the tap will only drip.

I write your absence into cold stone floors
and cornered light — a gull trapped
in the courtyard while it won't get dark,
her beak stretched wide, screaming for water.

Matryoshka Dolls

St. Petersburg

Trembling in crowded rows, the little dolls
present their bright, hand-painted faces
to the tourists in the square. Shoulder to shoulder,
the sellers' carts transform to crooked halls
recalling dark-choked clutter, attic places
that I groped through as a child. Here, older,

I grab a new friend's shirtsleeve like a little girl,
fearing the swarm of bodies in the square,
even the murky sky, could suck us in.
Smile fixed as a mask, the vendor curls
some bills around her sweaty fingers as I stare
into the hull each shrinking doll has been.

The salesgirl doesn't tell us how the wood,
cut every April when the sap still runs,
is left two years outside to dry, or how,
bent at his lathe, the craftsman turns a girlhood
so precise that every clean bisection stuns
and neatly recollects its parts. With him now,

alone in this strange country, this big crowd,
I split one blue-eyed, scarf-clad maiden down
until her body is no larger than a pea.
I hand my rubles to the vendor, but it's too loud
to piece together what she's said. Only her frown
among the lacquered grins remembers me.

Whale Song

Mary Starbuck: daughter of a whaling captain, poet, author, founding secretary of the Nantucket Historical Society.

The sea still wonders where they've gone.
Oil lamps burn a clean light, dim in the streets.

I walk, half-sleeping, to the open-shut percussion
of raked scallop shells, piled blinking in their salty hut.

Once, my father brought me home a drum of pickled limes.
One rolls small and green in the night sky of my belly.

But where have they gone? Nobody listens.
Young dockhands drown their eyes and search the latticework.

Low tide still stinks of eelgrass drying.
Sometimes I see whales passing by, strung black against the moon.

From the widow's walk, I look for clues in constellations.
A thousand-year box holds loose ends, but no bones for me to stee

High up, the great boat is luffing. Its astral sails slap
the dark in a slow turn. It drags a harpoon in its wake.

As a girl, I tied a piece of muslin to the railing on the roof.
It shows me the home of the wind.

The winter stalks like shadow, gray with sleet, ice-glare
sharp from streets that mirror silver sky. We search it.

The Atlantic doesn't freeze, but stares, slate-dark on paler distance.
If she knows now, she will not tell, swelling deep sighs while they breach

somewhere in a darkness I can't fathom, pierced by stars.

IV. Return

The Swimming Hole

We started out with all our clothes.
There was no moon. The crowded dark
invited us to spread along
the water's edge. I dipped my toes,
and noticed that I made no mark.
It wasn't cold — the man was wrong

to tell us, buying cigarettes,
It's almost fall, but fall implied
an end that we weren't ready for,
so we ignored him, making bets
on who'd be last. I stood beside
you drinking rum. The day before

we had all piled inside your jeep
with mud-caked shoes, pretending we
had longer. Here, I watched you taking
off your shirt. I laughed to keep
from shaking, turned so they would see
I'd done it too. Our bodies breaking

white above the glassy pond,
I saw us swimming out into
what seemed like nothing. Guided by
the cigarettes we held like wands,
we struggled forward, three-limbed, knew
it was the last time we would try.

Wedding Day

for Cally

The just-cut grass shivers with morning rain,
and all around the house, horse flies
and swallows drone and flit. How tightly the vein
presses the wrist's pale skin without disguise

or reticence — no matter how the waist
is cinched, the nervous thighs concealed in tulle
and satin skirts, the heart cocooned in spools
of silk and quarantined in lace.

The fly shadows the kitchen's hanging lights.
Burning his feet, he sticks, buzzes, and zooms.
Pruned tidily and flecked with bites,
the antique roses drift beside these quiet rooms.

All that we love here sprouts, blooms, scatters, and dies.
Today, the happy swallow dips and flies.

Metronome

Years after the piano tuner came last
and at last convinced us

that the sound had gone out
of the strings, the bass bridge,

and long after the sheet music
was shoved in the seat of the bench —

Christmas carols and scales, minuets
played for hours in a room

overshadowed by lilacs — after the upright
was rolled out of the house

as we readied to sell, the beat-keeper
still looks from the mantle.

So many minutes stand dumb
to the pendulum tock

of the old-fashioned instrument left
out for show. The unruly notes

are swept up, the melodies I learned
by heart. This gadget now measures

only in intervals of hush,
and like the emptied house

keeps counsel by itself, listens
        inside somewhere from a dark corner

where the lull has set, and where
        I can’t remember the time, the music.

Yule

The Holly King has won for now.
The year is old, and when it breaks
like icicles onto the walk,
we will not try to pry the boughs

up where their arches freeze into the ground.
Sunlight is meted out through paper
windows opening to laughter
rendered pocket-scale, to the sound

of dry leaves rasping on the glass,
the kettle hissing to a morning
built of frost, this season born
to grieve: what's past is past.

Midwinter

for my mother

Today you'll help your pagan friend lift her dead
dog's body to the highest branches of a maple tree.
On the phone, you tell me it's *the solstice* — I should *be ready*.

Today the light is shortest, and it's telling
me to hurry as I sort the bottles to recycle —
glass and plastic, slivered green. Your friend won't sell

her house that's falling down, or spend the time
to fix it, but you'll help her put her mind to rest
in bare limbs, closer to sky, the sun's climb

already finished when I go outside to shovel
snow from off the car, and bring the paper in.
I won't tell you that I haven't found a way to love

so I don't waste, or scrape the bottom — the granite step
against the shovel blade, the year creaked shut
with nothing gleaned. The women in our family kept

the early frost from killing gardens, fenced
the planted beds with chicken wire to keep
the rabbits out in spring. No measures left against

the time or weather as this year ends, you try to somehow mak
it up. You'll trail what someone else believes,
and haul the dead weight up the bole. You'll take

what little light is left to do your work: to wrap
the bale-twine tight around the sagging bones, your boots
balanced on splayed branches, body braced above the gap.

North

Three minutes in, the switchback trail
has turned to rock. The roadside lupines
on our way here looked like girls
left waving at the docks, and leaning close,
the white birch shadows slant
down sharply towards the parking lot.

It is a long drop. We watch cars wind
slowly down the interstate and stretch
our tired limbs across the granite face.
Engines ring against the mountainsides
and go. Crouched on a flat outcrop,
the collie gives a single bark, paws at her nose.

I didn't ask, but driving back, he pulled
us over where the flowers reached mid-thigh,
and stood to watch me bend among them.
Shivering violet in our hands, they made the car
smell like that notch-trapped air, rustled
like gossips for a week above my countertop.

Epithalamion

Tucuman, Argentina
for Dawson and Natalia

You brought her halfway up the world to see
snow loading the fields, plowed into towering hedgerows,
softening the edges of photographs, of roads.
She swept small angels on the lawn you left
behind, lived six weeks in the rooms you'd visited
in sleep, in dreams of birch and fire smoke, cold
that leaves a body aching for the thaw.

Here, your vowels slow. Here, your tongue forgets
the syllables of winter. She is what catches
in the yard — a note that rounds the Southern Pole
and holds. She is the longer light when ours
grows old, the vow of warmer months, a song
that knows of spanning distances, of snow.

Lupines

By now the seedpods rattle on their stalks.
  Two months ago, we skimmed
our hands along the flowers' tops, and picked
  the tapered blooms on walks
we took up to the highway. Tawny-limbed
  from summer, we had tricked

ourselves to thinking it would last — the pink
  and lapis petals lighting
every room, the hay-tall fields, my freckles.
  The lupines gone, I think
about the young girl in the legend, fighting
  tears while she watched grackles

fleck the rainless sky, and climbed the hill
  to give up what she loved
most to the gods so they would send a storm.
  They heard, poured rain until
the dried-up earth turned green, were so moved
  by her slender form

upon the mountain that they scattered seed
  that blossomed overnight,
covered hillsides with the graceful flower.
  Its shaken husks will feed
the foragers in winter when the light
  frames every short hour

as it goes. The world braces for cold,
    turns brown and sheds its leaves.
The clouds above the road threaten to stay,
   the coming snow to hold.
Below our feet, the bonnet's roots weave
   delicate networks in the clay.

Keeping Bees

My mother kept the beehives in our backyard,
small-domed against the wall of trees. She wore
a nylon-netted veil, and walked out in evenings,
gripping cotton gloves and a round, shallow pan
to hold the combs she'd coax out from the dark buzz.
She said it was an art, and moved, smooth as solder,

keeping her breaths small while she reached
one arm into the swarm, as deep as her shoulder.
The worker bees sank into clover, and I watched
from high up on the stone ledge, knowing
the honey's taste laced with the drone of the bees
when they rose — a dark pall — while she smoked out

the hives, moved the swarm among billows and blue sky,
calm in her black gauze, ghosting past trees.
I'd never been stung, still whenever a bee hummed by,
looking for peonies or lily blooms, I ducked,
low to the grass, shrank like the dog under the table,
who feared a thunderstorm each time like he'd been struck.

I thought to the bee, *there's nothing for you here*,
and swatted it on, up to the garden or apple tree to find
nectar, to feed its queen and all her tiny rows of cells,
six sides each, sharp-brimmed with sting and sweet.
In winter, the hives stood snow-capped, slumped
under drooping pines. I wondered how bees slept,

if they died, small bodies curled stinger to sternum,
frozen, dry in their dry nest. In winter, my mother
would keep to her room, *not enough light*
she would say, while she harvested afternoons, steeped
long in the south-facing glass. On the bed, her body
curled into itself, small under goose down, steady in sleep.

Summer, near dark, the fireflies gathered,
and from deep in the lower field, the barred owl
summoned the last flutter of light. I stood, resolute
by the hive, but I would not lift my hand to the dark
gape, would not dip my finger. I remember
that ache — and years later, after the bees

had gone, my mother withdrawn from their keeping,
I would go out to the wood's edge, where the hives
stayed like ruins, spread by raccoons and snow thaw,
some overturned, two jutting out on their balks,
close to falling. I knelt low in the long grass
to see one, and bracing my eyes, lifted the roof

from the body. I imagined its cavity strewn still
with thorax and fore wing — now blackened
by frost, dried far from the daylight. I raked
the inside but could find only broken combs — open
faced, and vacant as robbed graves — with no movement,
no sound to trace up from the dark middle.

The Bat

Downstairs, above my writing desk, her body
flitted overhead without my knowing —
something moth-like, a momentary shadow
on the ceiling light, a breath. It took

six passes for her presence to take shape,
for me to look from where I bent to see
the furry underside, her brown wings beating,
silent, in this strange, narrow enclosure,

brushing neither the window nor the wall,
calm almost, as if she trusted something in kind
in here would free her, heard long before I opened
it the sudden door leading her back into the dark.

The Author

Chelsea Woodard's first collection, *Vellum*, was published by Able Muse Press in 2014. Her poems have appeared in *The Threepenny Review*, *Southwest Review*, *Blackbird*, *American Life in Poetry*, and elsewhere. She lives and teaches in New Hampshire.

www.ingramcontent.com/pod-product-compliance
Lightning Source LLC
Chambersburg PA
CBHW020612310726
48979CB00008B/1445/J

* 9 7 8 1 9 3 9 5 7 4 1 8 3 *